ACHIEVE LEVEL 3

Reading

BY RICHARD COOPER
AND SHIRLEY ARMER

RISING ★ STARS

Rising Stars UK Ltd., 76 Farnaby Road, Bromley, BR1 4BH
Website: www.risingstars-uk.com

Every effort has been made to trace copyright holders and obtain their permission for the use of copyright material. The authors and publishers will gladly receive information enabling them to rectify any error or omission in subsequent editions.

All facts are correct at time of going to press.

New Edition 2003
Published 2003
First published 2002
Text, design and layout © Rising Stars UK Ltd.

Editorial: Tanya Solomons
Design: Starfish Design for Print
Illustrations: copyright © Burville-Riley
Cover photo: copyright © Getty Images

Rising Stars are grateful to Jane Bovey of Warren Road Primary School for her help and advice on this new edition.

All rights reserved. No part of this publication may be reproduced, stored in a retrieval system, or transmitted, in any form by any means, electronic, mechanical, photocopying, recording or otherwise, without the prior permission of Rising Stars UK Ltd.

British Library Cataloguing in Publication Data
A CIP record for this book is available from the British Library.

ISBN 1-904591-28-0

Printed at Wyndham Gait, Grimsby, UK

Contents

How to use this book	4
Reading strategies	6
Question words	7
Keywords	8
Reading tasks	10
Speaking and listening	12

LOOKING AT TEXTS

Indexes and glossaries	14
Finding information from books	16
Keywords	18
Reading cues	20

COMPREHENSION

Comprehension	22
Inference and deduction	24
Star Story	26
Information texts	28
Poetry comprehension	30
Invitations	32

POINTS OF VIEW

Expressing a preference	34
Explaining your point of view	36

NOTES FOR PARENTS

General reading tips	38
Reading with your child	39
Difficulties with reading	40
Book lists and authors	41
Reading record	43
The Key Stage 1 Tests	44
Helping your child do well	46

ANSWERS

	48

How to use this book

Each topic is covered in a similar way.

1 **Introduction section** – This section tells you what your child needs to do to get a Level 3. It picks out what the key learning objective is and explains it simply.

2 **The question** – The question helps your child to 'learn by doing'. It is presented in a similar way to the SATs questions and gives you a real example to work with.

3 **The flow chart** – This shows the steps to use when completing questions.

4 **The Star Tips** – How to get to grips with each topic.

5 **The Star characters** – Reading Star is the character who takes the children through the book. He explains the concepts being covered and offers support and an encouraging word at the right time.

6 **Practice questions** – This is where the children have to do the work! Try each question using the technique explained in the flow chart and then check the answers at the back.

What we have included:

We have included all the content that children will cover at Level 3 and may appear in the tests. This means you know that you are covering the main topics that will come up in the tests.

We have also included all the answers to the practice questions!

GOOD LUCK!

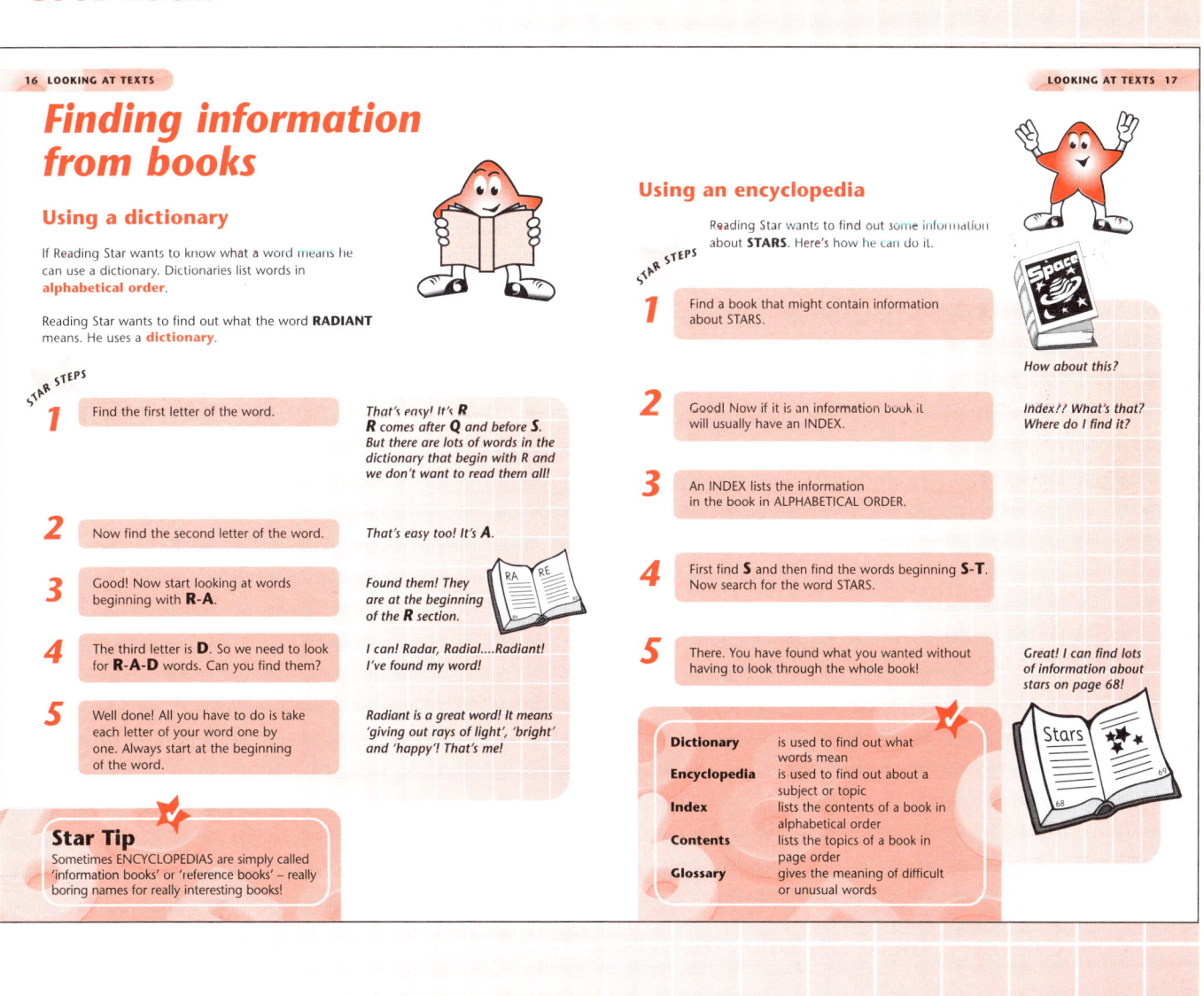

---

16 LOOKING AT TEXTS · LOOKING AT TEXTS 17

Finding information from books

Using a dictionary

If Reading Star wants to know what a word means he can use a dictionary. Dictionaries list words in **alphabetical order**.

Reading Star wants to find out what the word **RADIANT** means. He uses a **dictionary**.

STAR STEPS

1 Find the first letter of the word.

That's easy! It's **R**. **R** comes after **Q** and before **S**. But there are lots of words in the dictionary that begin with R and we don't want to read them all!

2 Now find the second letter of the word.

That's easy too! It's **A**.

3 Good! Now start looking at words beginning with **R-A**.

Found them! They are at the beginning of the **R** section.

4 The third letter is **D**. So we need to look for **R-A-D** words. Can you find them?

I can! Radar, Radial....Radiant! I've found my word!

5 Well done! All you have to do is take each letter of your word one by one. Always start at the beginning of the word.

Radiant is a great word! It means 'giving out rays of light', 'bright' and 'happy'! That's me!

Star Tip
Sometimes ENCYCLOPEDIAS are simply called 'information books' or 'reference books' – really boring names for really interesting books!

Using an encyclopedia

Reading Star wants to find out some information about **STARS**. Here's how he can do it.

STAR STEPS

1 Find a book that might contain information about STARS.

How about this?

2 Good! Now if it is an information book it will usually have an INDEX.

Index?? What's that? Where do I find it?

3 An INDEX lists the information in the book in ALPHABETICAL ORDER.

4 First find **S** and then find the words beginning **S-T**. Now search for the word STARS.

5 There. You have found what you wanted without having to look through the whole book!

Great! I can find lots of information about stars on page 68!

Dictionary	is used to find out what words mean
Encyclopedia	is used to find out about a subject or topic
Index	lists the contents of a book in alphabetical order
Contents	lists the topics of a book in page order
Glossary	gives the meaning of difficult or unusual words

Reading strategies

Strategies are the skills you use to help you do something. Learn your star strategies for reading. These strategies help you work out words you do not know.

Pictures

Use the pictures. They are there to help you.

Context

Context means using what you already know about the story to help you work out a word correctly.

Grammar

This is using the way the sentence is written to understand what the sentence means. If you get stuck on a word, try reading the whole sentence to see if it makes sense.

Keywords

Learn your keywords. The first 100 words make up three-quarters of all reading, so it makes sense to know these words by sight.

Using sounds

In reading we call sounds 'phonics'. Phonics are a very important part of learning to read. But remember – being able to use phonics is only one of the skills you need for reading. You must be able to use all of them.

Successful reader

Star Tip

When you have to stop and work out a word, always go back to the beginning of the sentence and re-read the whole thing. That way you don't lose the meaning.

Question words

When you are reading it is useful to know what you are looking for. Different questions start with different words. Have a look at these words and the examples we have given. If you know these words you can answer any question.

Who?

Who questions are asking about people or a person. They are mainly looking for a name or names.
Examples:
Who was the main character?
Who dropped the plate?

Where?

These questions are asking you to think about the places in the story or piece of writing.
Examples:
Where was the shoe when Finley found it?
Where was the story set?

What?

What questions are asking about the story and the things that have been happening.
Examples:
What was the first thing Jamie did?
What was the colour of Leo's jumper?

Why?

These are difficult questions. They are often asking you to read between the lines and give your own opinion.
Examples:
Why did Jamie reach into the box?
Why do you think Leo wore a yellow jumper?

When?

These questions are asking you to talk about time. Before, after, during, last week… are all good starting points for these answers.
Examples:
When did the story start?
When did Finley lose his shoes?

How?

How questions might need more than one answer. Think about the steps that might have happened.
Examples:
How did the boys get home?
How do you make toast?

Keywords

There are 150 keywords children should know by sight by the end of Year 2 and a further 88 words to learn by heart before the end of Year 4.

Learning keywords
★ Don't try to learn them all at once.
★ Learn a new set each week – about 10 words should be enough.
★ Keep revising the ones you have already learned.
★ Play games with the words to help you learn them, like bingo, snap or pelmanism (pairs).
You will need to write the keywords you are learning onto cards.

Tick each word in the list as you learn it!

☐ a	☐ boy	☐ first	☐ house	☐ may
☐ about	☐ brother	☐ for	☐ how	☐ me
☐ after	☐ but	☐ from	☐ I	☐ more
☐ again	☐ by	☐ get	☐ if	☐ much
☐ all	☐ call(ed)	☐ girl	☐ in	☐ mum
☐ am	☐ came	☐ go	☐ is	☐ must
☐ an	☐ can	☐ going	☐ it	☐ my
☐ and	☐ can't	☐ good	☐ jump	☐ name
☐ another	☐ cat	☐ got	☐ just	☐ new
☐ are	☐ come	☐ had	☐ last	☐ next
☐ as	☐ could	☐ half	☐ laugh	☐ night
☐ at	☐ dad	☐ has	☐ like	☐ no
☐ away	☐ day	☐ have	☐ little	☐ not
☐ back	☐ did	☐ he	☐ live(d)	☐ now
☐ ball	☐ dig	☐ help	☐ look	☐ of
☐ be	☐ do	☐ her	☐ love	☐ off
☐ because	☐ dog	☐ here	☐ made	☐ old
☐ bed	☐ don't	☐ him	☐ make	☐ on
☐ been	☐ door	☐ his	☐ man	☐ once
☐ big	☐ down	☐ home	☐ many	☐ one

KEYWORDS 9

☐ or	☐ see	☐ there	☐ want	☐ yes
☐ our	☐ seen	☐ these	☐ was	☐ you
☐ out	☐ she	☐ they	☐ water	☐ your
☐ over	☐ should	☐ this	☐ way	☐ days of the week
☐ people	☐ sister	☐ three	☐ we	☐ months of the year
☐ play	☐ so	☐ time	☐ went	☐ numbers up to 20
☐ plus	☐ some	☐ to	☐ were	☐ common colours
☐ pull	☐ take	☐ too	☐ what	☐ your name and address
☐ push	☐ than	☐ took	☐ when	
☐ put	☐ that	☐ tree	☐ where	
☐ ran	☐ the	☐ two	☐ who	
☐ said	☐ their	☐ up	☐ will	
☐ saw	☐ them	☐ us	☐ with	
☐ school	☐ then	☐ very	☐ would	

Now try this group of words.

☐ above	☐ change	☐ knew	☐ second	☐ under
☐ across	☐ coming	☐ know	☐ show	☐ until
☐ almost	☐ didn't	☐ leave	☐ sometimes	☐ upon
☐ along	☐ different	☐ might	☐ started	☐ used
☐ also	☐ does	☐ morning	☐ still	☐ walk(ed)(ing)
☐ always	☐ during	☐ near	☐ stopped	☐ watch
☐ any	☐ every	☐ never	☐ such	☐ while
☐ around	☐ following	☐ number	☐ suddenly	☐ without
☐ before	☐ found	☐ often	☐ think	☐ woke(n)
☐ began	☐ goes	☐ only	☐ thought	☐ write
☐ being	☐ gone	☐ opened	☐ through	☐ year
☐ below	☐ heard	☐ other	☐ today	☐ young
☐ better	☐ high	☐ outside	☐ together	
☐ between	☐ I'm	☐ place	☐ told	
☐ both	☐ inside	☐ right	☐ tries	
☐ brought	☐ jumped	☐ round	☐ turn(ed)	

Reading tasks

Try my Star Challenge!

Can you find something to read from each of these categories?

When you've read them, write down the titles here.

fiction book

newspaper

magazine

READING TASKS 11

How about these catagories? Can you find something to read from each of these?

When you've read them, write down the titles here.

comic

information book

recipe or instructions

Speaking and listening

Calling all star students! I hope you are listening carefully. Read through my checklist. It will help you develop all the key speaking and listening skills you need.

1 Talk and listen confidently

To help develop your confidence you could:

★ Act out a story you know with your friends. Each of you take the part of a character in the story.

★ Tell a younger child one of your favourite stories.

2 Share your ideas in discussions

Try having a debate with your friends.
Have a go at some of these questions.
Remember you have to say why you agree or disagree!

★ Should we have school uniform?

★ Would half days at school be better?

★ Who likes school dinners?

★ Which is the best football team?

★ Is Harry Potter better than Lord of the Rings?

Star Tip
You could talk about your reading book with someone in your family. This will help with speaking and listening too!

3 Think about the audience

The audience means 'who you are speaking to'.

Different audiences should be spoken to in different ways. How would you speak to

- ★ **your teacher...** very politely?
- ★ **your dad...** quietly?
- ★ **your friend...** having a chat?
- ★ **a baby...** using simple words?

4 Use Standard English

Standard English means making sure your sentences a

So, say:

- ★ **I did it** not I done it
- ★ **We were** not We was

Star Tip
Try to learn a new word every day to increase your vocabulary. Reading lots of books really helps with this.

Star Tip
Try watching the news. Imagine you were one of the people being interviewed. How would you answer the questions?

Indexes and glossaries

Time for more star skills and new words.
You need to practise your alphabet skills too.

Index

★ The index in a book helps you find what you are interested in without reading the whole book.

★ It gives you the page numbers to find.

★ It is usually at the back!

★ It is in alphabetical order.

Glossary

★ A glossary helps you understand important words in a book.

★ It is a mini dictionary of important words.

★ It is usually at the back of the book.

★ It is listed in alphabetical order.

Practice questions

Fill in the missing letters to help you practise alphabetical order.

a b c _ e _ g h _ j

k _ m _ o p _ _ s _

u _ _ x _ _

Star Tip
Indexes save you a lot of time if you can learn how to use them.

Star Tip
If you can't find a word you want in the glossary, just use a dictionary.

LOOKING AT TEXTS 15

Finding a word or a subject in an index or glossary means you need alphabet skills, so it's time for some more practice!

Practice questions

1 Put these words in alphabetical order.

star   night   bright   sky   ship   strap

_____, _____, _____, _____, _____

capitals   answers   information   dictionary   questions   books

_____, _____, _____, _____, _____, _____

2 Now have a go at making your own glossary.

You need to find the definition for each word and write them in alphabetical order!

space, astronaut, lift-off, navigate, rocket, launch

_____
_____
_____
_____
_____

Star Tip

This section is all about alphabetical order. Know this and you are on top of the game!

16 LOOKING AT TEXTS

Finding information from books

Using a dictionary

If Reading Star wants to know what a word means he can use a dictionary. Dictionaries list words in **alphabetical order**.

Reading Star wants to find out what the word **RADIANT** means. He uses a **dictionary**.

STAR STEPS

1 Find the first letter of the word.

*That's easy! It's **R**. **R** comes after **Q** and before **S**. But there are lots of words in the dictionary that begin with R and we don't want to read them all!*

2 Now find the second letter of the word.

*That's easy too! It's **A**.*

3 Good! Now start looking at words beginning with **R-A**.

*Found them! They are at the beginning of the **R** section.*

4 The third letter is **D**. So we need to look for **R-A-D** words. Can you find them?

I can! Radar, Radial....Radiant! I've found my word!

5 Well done! All you have to do is take each letter of your word one by one. Always start at the beginning of the word.

Radiant is a great word! It means 'giving out rays of light', 'bright' and 'happy'! That's me!

Star Tip
Sometimes ENCYCLOPEDIAS are simply called 'information books' or 'reference books' – really boring names for really interesting books!

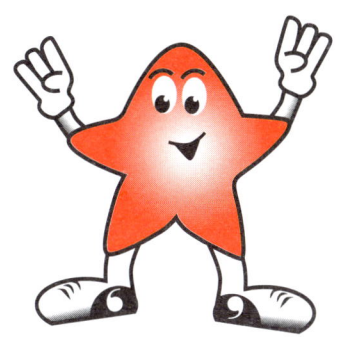

LOOKING AT TEXTS 17

Using an encyclopedia

Reading Star wants to find out some information about **STARS**. Here's how he can do it.

STAR STEPS

1 Find a book that might contain information about STARS.

How about this?

2 Good! Now if it is an information book it will usually have an INDEX.

Index?? What's that? Where do I find it?

3 An INDEX lists the information in the book in ALPHABETICAL ORDER.

4 First find **S** and then find the words beginning **S-T**. Now search for the word STARS.

5 There. You have found what you wanted without having to look through the whole book!

Great! I can find lots of information about stars on page 68!

Dictionary	is used to find out what words mean
Encyclopedia	is used to find out about a subject or topic
Index	lists the contents of a book in alphabetical order
Contents	lists the topics of a book in page order
Glossary	gives the meaning of difficult or unusual words

LOOKING AT TEXTS

Keywords

Star readers use scanning to search for keywords and answer comprehension questions.
Have a go!

Scanning means looking back at the passage to find words that are connected with the question.

Keywords are usually in the question. You look for them in the text to help you find the answer.

STAR STEPS

1 Read the passage carefully.

2 Remember to re-read any sentences where you paused for difficult words. — *That way you don't lose the meaning.*

3 Read the question very carefully. — *Double-check what it is asking you to find out.*

4 Which are the keywords? — *Scan the text for keywords.*

5 Read the part of the passage with the keyword. — *You should find your answer there.*

LOOKING AT TEXTS 19

Practice questions

**Practise finding the keyword.
Fill in the spaces.**

1 Anne saw Tom playing football.

Question: **What was Tom playing?**

(Keyword: **playing**)

Answer: **football**

2 They watched the mouse eat the cheese.

Question: **What did the mouse eat?**

(Keyword: _____)

Answer: _____

3 The match was cancelled due to rain.

Question: **Why was the match cancelled?**

(Keyword: _____)

Answer: _____

4 Jasmine fell asleep in class.

Question: **What did Jasmine do in class?**

(Keyword: _____)

Answer: _____

Star Tip
Check, check and check again.
★ The text
★ The keyword
★ The question
★ How many answers are needed?

20 LOOKING AT TEXTS

Reading cues

Cues are just clues that help you to read! You need to use all the clues to help you when you see a word that you do not know.

Question: Can you work out the missing word in this sentence?

The boat is f_____ on the water.

1 Look at the picture. — Always look at the pictures first. Can you guess the word?

2 Try the first sound. — Say the first sound. Try:
Fin?
Fish?
Flat?
Float?

3 Read on in the passage. — The rest of the sentence might tell you the word.

4 Re-read. — Go back and try the whole sentence again. Listen to which word would make sense.
The boat is float on the water.
OR
The boating is floating on the water.

5 Sound it out. — *If all else fails, sound out the whole word: f, l, oa, t, ing*

Star Tip
Remember – it's alright to guess, if your guess makes sense!

Star Tip
If you have to sound out a word, always re-read the sentence so as not to lose the meaning.

Practice questions

Can you find the missing words in these sentences?

1 The girl had toothache b_____ she ate too many sweets.

2 Blackbeard the pirate b_____ his gold on this island.

3 Waves sp_____ over the cliffs.

4 Tom tripped and dr_____ his crisps all over the floor.

5 This is the r_____ for chocolate fudge cake.

6 I r_____ a letter this morning.

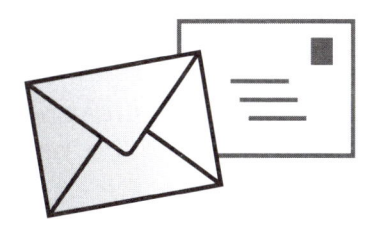

7 Miss Cooper had to speak in a w_____ as she had lost her voice.

8 The king's crown was covered with p_____ jewels.

9 The dragon b_____ the whole forest to the ground.

10 Mum tucked into a bag of her f_____ sweets.

Comprehension

Learning to read is probably the most important thing you will learn at Primary School.
It is the **key** to success – good readers unlock the door to learning!

Comprehension

The word comprehension means **understanding**. Reading without understanding is a waste of time.

Different types of writing

During the next few pages, you will be asked to complete comprehension questions on different types of writing:

Story

Operation Achieve

★ A story about the Star Crew going into action!

Information

Stars and Types

★ Information and facts about different types of stars.

Poetry

My Family Are Animals!

★ A poem about a child's family.

Invitations

Reading Star's birthday invitation

★ Find out all about Reading Star's birthday party.

Recipe

Star Topper

★ Find out how to make this delicious dish!

Different types of comprehension questions

There are different types of question you might be asked. Here are some tips for answering the questions. Use them to help you with the practice comprehensions.

RTQ – Do you know what this means? Look at the bottom of the page for the answer.

Multiple choice questions
★ Read these carefully.
★ How many choices are you being asked to make? You may be asked to tick **two** instead of one!
★ Always tick a box – even if you don't know the answer, it is better to have a guess.

Short answers
★ You may have to write one word or phrase to answer these. Make sure it's the correct one.
★ Use your scanning skills to find keywords.

Longer answers
★ There will be a bigger box to write in for these.
★ They may ask for your **opinion** – what you think and why.
★ These questions are worth the most marks.

How the questions help you
★ Some questions will tell you which page the answer is on.
★ Other questions may tell you which line the answer is on – especially in poems.

Drawing lines to the correct answer
★ Some types of question may ask you to match words or phrases by drawing lines from one to another.
★ Make sure your lines are clear.
★ Check your answer by re-reading what you've done.

Symbols
★ Remember to read symbols correctly.
★ For example, g is for grams and m is for metres.

RTQ = **R**ead **T**he **Q**uestion (always read it again!)

Inference and deduction

Reading Star likes to think that there are two types of comprehension question: 'bread and butter' questions and 'jam' questions!

Bread and butter questions are the easy ones. You need to get these ones right to do OK in a test.

The **jam** questions are harder – learn how to do these and you will do really well in a test! They often start with 'why'.

The bread and butter questions will be **deduction** style questions. The jam questions will be **inference** style questions.

★ Deduction – the answer will be right there in front of you.
★ Inference – you have to 'read between the lines' or look for clues within the text. The clues are there; you have to find them.

Practice questions

Have a look at these sentences. Each one has a 'bread and butter' (deduction) and a 'jam' (inference) question.

1 The cat ended up on Granny's lap and purred loudly.

Bread and butter – Where did the cat curl up?

"On Granny's lap." It says so in the sentence.

Jam – How do you think the cat felt? Why?

Happy and contented, because cats purr when they are happy and contented.

Practice questions

2 Alice put on her mermaid costume and set off with the dolphin to the party.

Bread and butter – What costume did Alice wear?

> Alice wore a mermaid costume. "Costume" is a keyword here.

Jam – What sort of party was Alice going to?

> A fancy dress party. It doesn't actually say so in the sentence but from all the clues you would say that it was a fancy dress party. Use keywords like "mermaid costume" and "dolphin".

3 Harry trembled as he stepped off the Ghost Train ride.

Bread and butter – What ride had Harry been on?

> Use the keyword "ride". Now scan the text – it was the Ghost Train ride.

Jam – Why do you think that Harry was trembling?

> It doesn't actually say so but the phrase "Harry trembled" suggests he was scared, probably by something in the Ghost Train.

Star Tip

Remember to read the question and work out whether it's a bread and butter or jam one!

Star Story
Operation Achieve

The Star Crew held their breath. Reading Star looked a little nervous but he always did just before a jump. The Starship hovered above Valley School, holding its position in the strong breeze that was beginning to blow in from the west.

'Three... two... one.... Shooting Stars!' yelled the crew as they threw themselves out of the Starship and into the warm night air. Reading Star looked up as his parachute burst open and he just caught a glimpse of the other two Stars below him, their canopies reflecting the moonlight.

All three Stars landed safely in the school playground. As they looked up, they could just see the Starship as it sped back to base, disappearing over the fence and tall trees that marked the boundary of the school grounds.

Maths Star was the first to speak.

'An excellent landing. We leapt from the Starship at an angle of 60 degrees and opened our 'chutes after 2.5 seconds. By my calculations we have hit our target! Well done team!'

Writing Star nodded in agreement. He wasn't going to admit that he had kept his eyes closed all the way down.

Reading Star was much calmer now and spoke firmly to his companions.

'Fellow Stars. We have a job to do. Valley School needs us and we must not let them down. Let's go!'

With that the three little Stars formed a cluster and shouted their battle cry – 'Achieve for one and achieve for all!' – before running as fast as they could towards the shadows of the school building. In their haste, not one of them noticed the little satchel packed full of 'Star Tips' that Reading Star had left behind in the playground...

Questions

The first few questions are the 'bread and butter' or deduction questions. The next few are the 'jam' questions. These are inference style questions.

Bread and butter questions

1 Which Star looked nervous?

Maths Star ☐

Writing Star ☐

Reading Star ☐

2 What is the name of the school in the story?

3 Which two things marked the edge of the school grounds? (tick two)

a stream ☐   a building ☐

tall trees ☐   a fence ☐

Starship base ☐

4 From which direction was the wind blowing?

5 What is the Star Crew battle cry?

Jam questions

1 Which two stars jumped from the Starship first?

2 How do you know?

3 Do you think the Star Crew had done this before?

Yes ☐   No ☐

4 Explain your answer.

5 Why do you think the Star Crew jumped at night?

6 Why wouldn't Writing Star admit to keeping his eyes closed all the way down?

7 What do you think the Star Crew was going to do at Valley School?

Information texts

Stars and Types

Stars have lives and are born like people. The lifetime of a star is much longer than ours! A star is born when huge, thick clouds of dust and gas in space begin to collapse under their own weight. The gas then explodes and the young star starts to shine.

When you look at a starry sky you can see that some stars are brighter than others. Some stars twinkle too. Twinkling is caused by the Earth's atmosphere, which is constantly moving.

People have always liked to imagine that stars make up patterns and pictures, called constellations. Many constellations were invented by the Babylonians and passed on by the Ancient Greeks and Romans. This is why astronomers use Latin names for constellations.

The nearest star to Earth is our Sun, which is 93 million miles away! The light from our Sun takes eight minutes to reach the Earth. The next nearest star is Proxima Centauri, which is 25 million, million miles away.

Shooting stars aren't actually stars at all. They are small fragments of rock that whizz towards Earth from space. They burn up when they enter our atmosphere and light up the sky for a split second.

Questions

1. What happens when huge thick clouds of dust and gas begin to collapse in space?

   ✏️ _____ and _____

2. How long does it take for the Earth to receive the Sun's light?

   ✏️ _____

3. What is a pattern or picture made of stars called?

   ✏️ _____

4. What does the Earth's atmosphere seem to cause stars to do when we look at them?

   ✏️ _____

5. Shooting stars aren't stars at all?   True ☐   False ☐
   Explain your answer.

   ✏️ _____

6. Fill in the table to show which statements about Stars and Types are fact and which are opinion. Tick the correct box.

	Fact	Opinion
The Sun is a star		
The Babylonians knew all about stars		
These facts are amazing!		
The second nearest star to Earth is Proxima Centauri		
Seeing a shooting star brings you good luck		

Star Tip
Look at each statement in turn and ask if they can be proved by evidence in the Stars and Types section.

Poetry comprehension

My Family Are Animals!

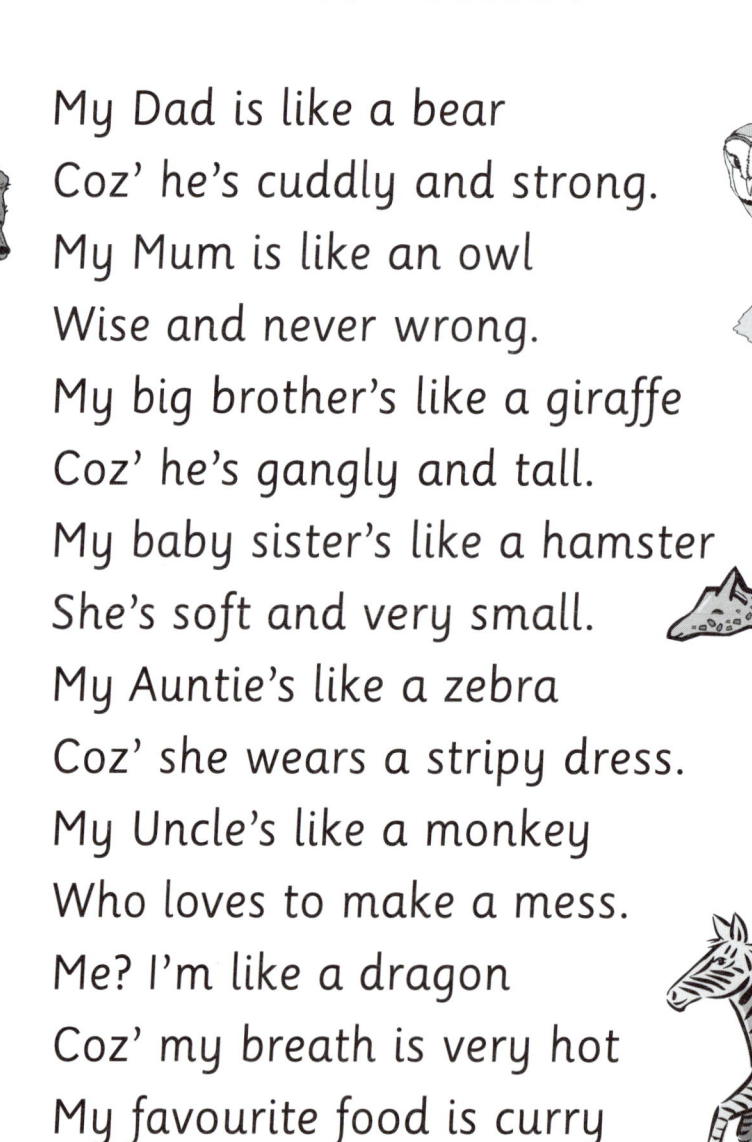

My Dad is like a bear
Coz' he's cuddly and strong.
My Mum is like an owl
Wise and never wrong.
My big brother's like a giraffe
Coz' he's gangly and tall.
My baby sister's like a hamster
She's soft and very small.
My Auntie's like a zebra
Coz' she wears a stripy dress.
My Uncle's like a monkey
Who loves to make a mess.
Me? I'm like a dragon
Coz' my breath is very hot
My favourite food is curry
Of which I eat a lot.

COMPREHENSION 31

Read the poem '**My Family Are Animals!**'

Questions

1 What sort of animal would you be?

2 Why?

When we say something is *like* something else it is called a **simile**.
Similes are a great to use in poems!

3 Can you write a simile for these examples? The first one has been done for you.

The sun is *like* a gold medal for the sky.

The sea is *like*

The moon is *like*

The mountain is *like*

The head-teacher is *like*

My best friend is *like*

Read the poem 'My Family are Animals!' again.

4 Make a list of the pairs of words that rhyme.

strong and wrong

5 Did you like the poem?

I liked this poem *because*…
or I didn't like this poem *because*…

COMPREHENSION

Invitations

I invited all of my friends to my birthday party. It was great fun – everybody came in fancy dress.

Here is the invitation that I sent out.

INVITATION

You are invited to **Reading Star's** birthday party.

At: **The Starship**
On: **Saturday 29th February**
From: **2:00pm** to **6:00pm**

The party will be fancy dress and the theme will be **sea creatures.**

Please reply to:
The Starship
Above the clouds
Near the Moon
SP1 0RB

By 28th February

Questions

1 Where was the party being held?

The Moon ☐   The Starship ☐   Under the Sea ☐

2 What day of the week was the party?

3 How long did the party last?

2 hours ☐   4 hours ☐   6 hours ☐

4 The party was fancy dress. What did the guests have to dress up as?

spaceships ☐   moon monsters ☐   sea creatures ☐

5 What is the Starship's postcode?

Recipes

Here is the recipe for my favourite snack. It is called the 'Star Topper'.

Star Topper
Ingredients

1 slice of thick brown bread
1 small tin of baked beans
1 egg
50g of grated cheddar cheese
butter
dash of Worcester sauce

Materials

Grill
Toaster
Saucepan
Frying pan
Grater
Knife

Method

1. Heat up the grill.
2. Toast the bread in the toaster.
3. While the bread is toasting, heat the beans in the saucepan.
4. Next, fry the egg in a little butter until lightly cooked.
5. Butter the toast and place the fried egg on top.
6. Pour the beans around the egg leaving the yolk clear.
7. Sprinkle the grated cheese around the yolk and place under the grill until the cheese is bubbling.
8. Add a dash of Worcester sauce and enjoy!

WARNING
Always ask an adult to help you when cooking food.

Star Tip
Read each question carefully, especially number 3!

Questions

1. How many grams of cheese should you use?

2. What should you do while the bread is toasting?

3. What is the butter used for? (tick 2 boxes)

   Buttering the bread ☐

   Mixing with the beans ☐

   Frying the egg ☐

   To help the cheese bubble under the grill ☐

4. What is the last ingredient to be added?

5. The snack is called a 'Star Topper'. Do you think this is a good name for it? Explain your answer.

Expressing a preference

Sometimes you may be asked what you think about something. It is no good just saying whether you like it or not – you have to say WHY. The word **because** is very useful here!

I like strawberries and cream **because** they remind me of summer.

Or

I didn't enjoy that film very much **because** the monster was too scary!

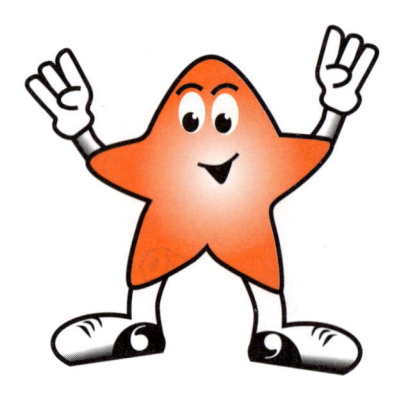

Write about your favourite things using the hints below.

What is your favourite book?

My favourite book is

Why?

Because

What do you enjoy most at school?

I enjoy

Why?

Because

POINTS OF VIEW 35

Which food do you like eating the best?

I like eating _____

Why?

Because _____
_____

Do you like playing with teddy bears?

I _____ like playing with teddy bears.

Why?

Because _____
_____

What do you like watching on television?

I like watching _____

Why?

Because _____
_____

Do you like helping with jobs around the home?

I _____ helping with jobs around the home.

Why?

Because _____
_____

Star Tip

Try not to use the word 'nice'. Think of other words that describe how you feel.

Explaining your point of view

If you want to explain what you think and say, it helps if you can **back up** what you are saying with FACTS and REASONS.

Point of view

Elephants don't make good pets.

Facts or reasons

★ They are too big to fit in a house.
★ They eat too much food.
★ They need a big space to exercise in.
★ They are 'wild' animals that need their freedom.

Now it's your turn!

All schools should have a heated swimming pool.

POINTS OF VIEW 37

Children who live nearby should always walk to school in the morning.

Tigers are dangerous animals so they should be killed whenever possible.

The sea is huge so it's a good place to dump our rubbish.

Star Tip
Give your opinion first and then try to explain it. Remember the words 'Why?' and 'Because'. Always give REASONS.

General reading tips

To become a reading superstar a child needs lots of positive support. Each child needs to be able to read with confidence, fluency and understanding. Parents can play a vital role in helping their children.

Star Tips for parents

★ **Read to your child every day!**
Hearing a skilled reader read helps children with their own reading and writing.

It allows them to experience books that would be too difficult for them to manage alone.

It broadens their vocabulary and increases the imaginative detail they can bring to their own writing.

★ **Help children to read their own books.**
Remember, reading is not a test and a child who enjoys and loves books will find learning to read much easier.

Make their reading time pleasant and stress free!

★ **Talk about the pictures.**
Learning to interpret the illustrations in a book is a key skill at this stage.

★ **Discuss what you read in detail.**
Ask what your child thinks will come next.

Ask them to retell significant parts of a story to you.

Ask them why they think something happened or a character acted as they did.

★ **Read a variety of texts with them.**
Try reading poems, newspapers, comics, recipes, instructions, maps and timetables.

Reading with your child – asking questions

To help your child get the most out of their reading books, encourage them to talk about the story as they are reading.

You can ask these questions when reading stories with your child:

★ **Look at the title and the cover. What do you think this book is going to be about?**

★ **Do the first few pages of the book make you want to carry on reading it? Why?**

★ **How do you think the story will end?**

★ **What do you think might happen next?**

★ **Why do you think the book is called…?**

★ **Can you tell me what has happened so far?**

★ **Which part of the story do you think is the funniest/saddest/most interesting? Why do you think that?**

★ **Who was your favourite character? What did you like about them?**

★ **Did the book make you think of something that has happened to you?**

★ **Do the pictures help you understand the book better? How?**

★ **Are the pictures clear? Do they make the book more enjoyable?**

★ **Is the book set out in an unusual way?**

Also ask questions that are specific to each story about what is happening and why. 'Why…?' questions are particularly good for getting children to think about the story and checking their understanding.

Difficulties with reading

If your child is having difficulty with reading, talk to the school. They will give you advice.

Here are some strategies that may help you at home:

★ Take the pressure off – make reading time relaxed and comfortable.

★ Write a simple book together, e.g. Our Day Out, My Birthday, Football.

★ Encourage your child to notice words around them in the environment – on cereal packets, road signs, shops and so on.

★ Take it in turns to read a sentence or page.

★ Read **to** them and just let them read the occasional word.

★ Read a passage through to them first and then let them have a go.

★ Make sure the books they are reading are at the right level. So, if the book has 100 words in it you should expect them to know at least 95 words. This is a comfortable level of difficulty that will maintain their confidence.

★ Try reading different materials, such as comics, magazines, instructions for toys, recipes, poems or joke books.

★ Find them a book about something they are interested in.

Book lists and authors

There are many excellent books that will interest your child. The list below provides some suggestions to start you off.

Don't forget, your local library will have a huge selection of reading material for your child to choose from and it's all free!

Picture books for more able readers

On The Way Home by Jill Murphy (Macmillan Children's Books)

Worried Arthur by Joan Stimson (Ladybird Books)

Mrs Lather's Laundry by Allan Ahlberg (Puffin Books)

Beware of Boys by Tony Blundell (Puffin Books)

Curtis the Hip Hop Cat by Gini Wade (Macmillan Children's Books)

Floss by Kim Lewis (Walker Books)

The Paperbag Princess by Robert N Munsch (Scholastic)

Mog the Forgetful Cat by Judith Kerr (Picture Lions)

Bringing the Rain to Kapiti Plain by Verna Aardema (Macmillan Children's Books)

The Clothes Horse and Other Stories by Janet and Allan Ahlberg (Puffin Books)

The Monster Bed by Jeanne Willis (Red Fox)

Dinosaurs and all that Rubbish by Michael Foreman (Longman)

The Ice Palace by Angela McAllister and Angela Barrett (Red Fox)

Katie Morag Stories by Mairi Hedderwick (Red Fox)

Jafta by Hugh Lewin (Collins)

Jyoti's Journey by Helen Ganly (Andre Deutsch)

Dr Xargle's Book of Earthlets by Jeanne Willis and Tony Ross (Red Fox)

There are many non-fiction books to choose from. Go for books that are not overloaded with print and have clear and well-labelled pictures and diagrams.

Star Tip
Remember – it's important for children to hear books being read aloud **to** them!

42 NOTES FOR PARENTS

Early chapter books

Blue Banana Series (Egmont Books)

Emily's Legs by Dick King-Smith (Hodder Wayland)

SuperDad the Super Hero by Shoo Rayner (Hodder Wayland)

Boys Are Us by Shoo Rayner (Collins)

Orson Cart Saves Time by Steve Donald (Red Fox)

Help! I'm A Dinosaur by Colin Tulloch and John Richardson (Straw Hat)

Pappy Mashy by Kathy Henderson (Walker Books)

"Do I Look Funny to You?" by Nicola Matthews (Bloomsbury)

Lily the Lost Puppy by Jenny Dale (Macmillan Children's Books)

Space Race by Malorie Blackman (Corgi Pups)

E.S.P. by Dick King-Smith (Andre Deutsch)

Omnibombulator by Dick King-Smith (Young Corgi)

Star's Turn by Linda Newbery (Corgi Pups)

Free the Whales by Jamie Rix (Walker Books)

Great Shot by Rob Childs (Corgi)

Intermediate chapter books

Bing Bang Boogie It's a Boy Scout by Bob Wilson (Collins)

Mossycoat by Phillip Pullman (Scholastic Hippo)

The Goose Girl by Gillian Cross (Scholastic Hippo)

The Twelve Dancing Princesses by Anne Fine (Scholastic Hippo)

Aesop's Fables by Malorie Blackman (Scholastic Hippo)

The Amazing Pet by Marjorie Newman (Corgi)

The Magic Finger by Roald Dahl (Puffin)

I'm Scared by Bel Mooney (Egmont)

The Julian Stories by Ann Cameron (Corgi)

Stinkers Ahoy! by Roger McGough (Galaxy)

You're Thinking About Doughnuts by Michael Rosen (Barn Owl Books)

Happy reading!

Reading record

Note
Use this lined paper for keeping a reading record. Jot down the titles of all the books you have read and include the author's name too.

The Key Stage 1 Tests

What are SATs?

The Key Stage 1 National Tests, or SATs as they are commonly known, are assessments that take place at the end of Year 2. There are tests in Reading, Writing and Maths and these are supported by Teacher Assessment in all three areas.

The tests are usually carried out during May and are spread out over several weeks to ease the pressure on the children. They take place as part of a normal day and most schools do not tell the children they are doing a 'test'. The children will have done plenty of practices and preparation in school and the tests are usually carried out in the classroom with the teacher.

What do the levels mean?

The National Curriculum sets down levels children are expected to reach by certain ages. On average children will be at

- Level 2 by the end of Key Stage 1 (age 7)
- Level 4 by the end of Key Stage 2 (age 11)
- Level 5/6 at the end of Key Stage 3 (age 14)

Within each level there are strands A, B and C where A indicates the child is working confidently within the level, B is average and C shows they are just achieving within the level.

What do the tests consist of?

Writing

There are two Writing Tasks, a Spelling Test and a Handwriting Task. The Writing Tasks consist of a longer task, which is usually in the form of a story, and a shorter task, which will take a different form, perhaps a letter or a set of instructions. The children will be expected to work independently and spell and punctuate their work as best they can. The tasks are not timed but it is expected that the longer task should take about 45 minutes and the shorter one about 30 minutes.

There is also a separate Spelling Test where children are required to write a list of words read out by the teacher. There are about 20 words and the majority of them will be words the children have already come across.

Handwriting is also looked at. In some cases handwriting is assessed as part of the Writing Tasks. Children might be asked to copy out a part of their story in their best handwriting and will be expected to join some letters.

Reading

The Reading Test consists of a reading task and a separate comprehension test. During the reading task the child will read part of a book to a teacher and should be able to discuss the book and answer questions. Their ability to work out unknown words, read with good pace and expression and show an understanding of the story are all assessed.

For the reading comprehension test the children are given a reading booklet with a story and piece of non-fiction writing in. The children will be expected to read as much as they can independently and answer the questions that are in the booklet.

Maths

All children will take a written Maths Test. It covers most aspects of Number and Shape, Space and Measuring. There are also some mental maths questions that the teacher will read out. There is an emphasis on Using and Applying mathematical knowledge and children are often asked to solve simple problems and explain their answers.

What is the Teacher Assessment?

At the end of Key Stage 1 teachers also carry out their own assessments of each child in the areas of Reading, Writing and Maths. These assessments are based on classroom observations and looking at a child's work over a period of time. Usually the Teacher Assessment level is the same as the SATs level but occasionally there are discrepancies. It is worth remembering that the SATs level is an indication of how your child performed on one particular day under test-like conditions and only covers small areas of the curriculum. The Teacher Assessment gives a more rounded view of the child's ability and covers all aspects of the English and Maths curriculums.

Helping your child do well

There is no right way to prepare your child and it is not necessary to spend hours revising for a test. Most children do not even know they are doing a test and this is the best preparation for them!

Most schools do not tell the children they are taking a test as this adds a huge amount of pressure on them to get it all right. They will have had opportunities to try practice papers, doing as much as they can independently. When the real test comes it is usually seen as just another classroom activity.

Working at home with your child

Working through these books with your child will help reinforce what they have learnt during Year 2 and get them used to answering test type questions. Here are some things you can do:

- Find time when you are both relaxed and happy.
- Choose a quiet spot without distractions.
- Keep sessions short, especially when you see your child is getting bored or frustrated.
- Work through examples in this book together and then allow your child to have a go at the practice questions. Read the *Star Tips* together – you could ask your child to come up with different voices for the characters!
- Encourage them if they find something difficult. Try not to let your frustrations show, as they will pick up on this and become more anxious themselves. Take a short break and try again tomorrow.
- Try to make all activities meaningful for them. When practising writing letters, why not write one to a friend or relative? This will encourage them to practise their reading when they get a reply! Or ask them to write out your shopping list for you. Let them play with your money and encourage them to work out totals and calculate change using real coins.

All children will find questions on the papers that they cannot do or find very challenging and some can find this hard to cope with. You can help by encouraging them to have a go at something difficult and not to give up when it gets tough. A challenging jigsaw puzzle is a good place to start.

Of course, preparation does not always have to take the form of pencil and paper work. Children learn by doing so try some fun practical activities:

- **Read to your child. This will help greatly with their writing as they learn about story structure and acquire new vocabulary.**
- **Ask your child to tell you a bedtime story for a change.**
- **Play games. Board games such as snakes and ladders or dominoes are great for all those number skills. Use long car journeys for word games.**
- **Play shops with REAL money!**

Often children's concerns or worries about the tests come from parents' own concerns about their child. Unless your child's school tells the children they are doing a test, try not to talk to them, or in front of them, about the tests. Keep things as normal as possible during the test period and take opportunities to celebrate their success. A word of praise from a parent goes a long way!

Good luck and have fun!

Answers

Page 14

abc**def**gh**i**jk**l**m**n**op**qr**s**t**u**vw**x**yz**

Page 15
1) First set: bright, night, ship, sky, star, strap
   Second set: answers, books, capitals, dictionary, information, questions

2) astronaut, launch, lift-off, navigate, rocket, space. Definitions may vary.

Page 19
1) Keyword: playing Answer: football
2) Keyword: eat Answer: cheese
3) Keyword: cancelled Answer: it was raining
4) Keyword: class Answer: Jasmine fell asleep

Page 21
1) because
2) buried
3) sprayed
4) dropped
5) recipe
6) received
7) whisper
8) priceless
9) burned
10) favourite

Page 27
Bread and Butter questions
1) Reading Star
2) Valley School
3) Tall trees and a fence
4) The west
5) "Achieve for one and achieve for all!"

Jam questions
Explanations may vary.
1) Writing Star and Maths Star jumped first.
2) Reading Star could see the other parachutes below him.
3) Yes
4) They opened their parachutes quickly.
5) So no one would see them.
6) He didn't want Reading Star and Maths Star to know he was scared.
7) The Star Crew was going to help the children to learn.

Page 29
1) The gas explodes and a star begins to shine.
2) 8 minutes
3) A constellation
4) It causes stars to twinkle.
5) True. They are small fragments that burn up when they reach the Earth's atmosphere.
6) From the top: Fact, Fact, Opinion, Fact, Opinion

Page 31
1) Answers will vary
2) Answers will vary
3) Answers will vary
4) tall and small, dress and mess, hot and lot
5) Answers will vary

Page 32
1) The Starship
2) Saturday
3) 4 hours
4) Sea creatures
5) SP1 0RB

Page 33
1) 50 grams
2) Heat the beans in a saucepan.
3) Buttering the bread and frying the egg.
4) Worcester sauce

Page 35-37
Answers will vary on these pages but children should give reasons for their views.